When it happens to you…

When it happens to you...

Poems by Alice Teeter

When it happens to you . . .

Published by

~Star Cloud Press®~
6137 East Mescal Street
Scottsdale, Arizona 85254-5418

ISBN: 978-1-932842-35-7 — $12.95

Library of Congress Control Number: 2009921118

Printed in the United States of America

For Carroll Elder Teeter and his sister,
Martha Teeter Lawson Furnari Edwards,
two still living of those who raised me in such a way.

Table of Contents

II. Vibrations — The stars will come down…

VARIATIONS — WHAT WAS THAT LIKE?

For Becky, Ellen, David
& our "Replacements"

POEM FOR ELLEN

Whom did you know first, your mother or your twin?
Your mother was you, your twin yourself divided whole –
the egg that sat nestled in that red light, safe and warm,
waiting for the journey to begin.

Whom did you know best? That particle of matter swimming
in a vast sea alone – or the vibration, the wave that was all motion?
Who were you when you set off – that one –
that one become two become three?

And who knew you best? The chemistry that created you –
the blood you were born from, or the cell you left one day
in the dark – the being that was you, then two?

*   *   *

Who were you closest to? Your mother who held you
in her body growing or the you you were held with –
the two of you, forearms pushing against each other
in the hot stew that fed you and you –
that kept your bodies warm and your minds alive?

What was that like – to be born first, shoved out
alone and handled by substance you couldn't perceive
in an enormous rush of air? And what was that like –
to be left behind? Was it terrifying and luxurious,
all that space so suddenly yours alone?

1

DREAM 1: MY MOTHER WRITES POETRY...

My mother writes poetry I've never seen.
She writes in English and publishes only in Chinese journals.
For years I did not know she even wrote poetry.
Now I cannot find it.
The journals are obscure.
Thin, flimsy paper. The ink shows through from the other side.
Most of the journal is in Chinese.
Here and there will be the poems of my mother
and poems by other unknown poets.
The print is in two colors – red and black.
The poem titles are in red and the poems themselves print black.
I am amazed to be reading the poems of my mother.
I did not know she wrote poetry.
Most of her poems are lost to me.

Sometimes when I find one of those small Chinese party umbrellas,
I unroll the paper that makes up the shaft and look for her poems.
I have to be very careful to unroll it in one piece,
spread it out on a clean, flat surface, check it back and front.
When I am lucky I find a poem
and read the words of my mother's heart,
scattered among the hieroglyphs of another language,
printed in a country I have never seen.

I am ten years old again,
dancing in my body.
I own the world again.
What I create with my movement lives:
A horse running across a mountain meadow,
A bear on hind legs reaching for honey,
A burglar creeping through the night.
I am the spring breeze.
I start the tornado.
I crouch as a lion bloody over kill.
All these things flow from me.
All these things stir in my wake.

No wonder 10 year old girls
are so dangerous.
No wonder they must be hobbled,
and branded, tied up tight,
underfed and starving.

Here is my ten year old again.
She is ready to conjure the lion the bear the lamb.
She is ready to call the wolf the boar the snake.
She is ready to be the wild wild mare.

WOMAN,

Be a young man
step out
and fly fly fly
empty hands
wide heart
the world
spread out
ready for you
to pick up
a blue green marble
a coin you flip once
heads tails
you're off
no purse
no direction
no destination
no reason
just because

The Snake

You are walking down the street – a city street. You notice a large snake to your right – enormous – its girth is as high as your waist. It is so still you think it might be dead and you sniff the air to see if you can detect the odor of decay. You hear a rustle behind you, then a rattle, ahead you see the snake's head lash out to bite a young boy on the ankle.

You see the snake sliding down the hall toward your brother's open bedroom door. You see it glide up and over into the bottom drawer of his dresser. You know your brother is in his room. You do not know if he has seen the snake, so you go in to warn him just as the snake comes slithering out the open top drawer. Your brother grabs its head and yells for you to get something but you don't understand him. He gestures with his free hand and you realize he wants the padded envelope sitting on his desk, its end a row of jagged staples. He drops the snake tail first in the opening and you are both terrified it will rear up and bite, but it falls as if dead or asleep into the bottom of the envelope.

You carry the mailer outside. Your twin is there and she has pliers. She begins pulling out the jagged staples even though you are screaming at her over and over again to go get the goddamn staple gun. She takes a hammer and begins pounding nails into the padding at the end of the bag.

Your older sister stands nearby. She's smiling. She likes to see you yelling at your twin.

Your father stands apart. He's so old. He apologizes for being too weak and is sorry that he cannot help.

You look around at your brother standing in the front door swinging the screen door back and forth, his red striped shirt a little too small; your twin kneeling on the driveway hammer in hand, looking up at you with your own eyes; your older sister a little way down the pavement, her arms crossed, her glasses slipping down her nose; your father standing on the grass, his head bent in the warm sunlight, his arms wrapped around himself. You are all looking at each other, but everyone's attention is on the snake unmoving in the brown padded bag at your feet.

SHE WALKED THROUGH THE DOOR

looked around
said
"wait a minute"
and turned around to leave
but the door wasn't there anymore

SHE HAD A BEIGE CHILDHOOD.

Everything. Her mother dressed in beige.
Her mother dressed her in beige.
Beige ribbons, beige smocks, beige panties, beige socks.
Beige bedspread, beige walls, beige stationery, beige halls.
Only the bathroom was green.
She loved the bathroom going in and
staying for hours.
Consequently her beige mother soon ordered her
not to go into the bathroom
unless she absolutely had to.
She couldn't lie.
So she drank plenty and lots of water
and a few times of flooding her beige panties
convinced her mother.

If she will only admit it
she will be free.
If she will open her clothes
so we can see the truth,
she will walk out light-hearted.
If she would just let the sun
fall onto every little bit of skin
as she stands fully bare before us.

If she will only say "Yes, this is me,
all of me, every admirable and rotten bit"
and not obfuscate obliterate befog,

but she stands there throwing up Buddha,
a long, rambling essay on what she means,
buying shoes and forgetting.

If he will only admit it
he will be free.
If he will take off his clothes
so we can see all of him,
he will walk out buoyant.
If he would just let the sun
fall onto every pore, every wrinkle
as he stands uncovered before us.

ALICE TEETER

If he will only say "Yes, this is me,
all of me, every beautiful and nasty bit"
and not obfuscate obliterate befog,

but he stands there throwing up the Engineer,
a short, terse treatise on what he means,
drinking beer and forgetting.

I AM POISED AND READY FOR TAKE OFF.

I am ready to go.
I am all set to begin.
Everything is in place.
The dishes are done.
The bed is made.
The television is off.

I've fitted arrow to bow.
I've cleared out the in.
I've washed my face.
The bills are all paid.
I've hunted high and low.

I've forgiven my sin.
I've made a space.
The letters are weighed.
The top is aspin.

11

STRING THEORY

For Jo

oh.
Oh,
OH !
Here I am.
When I was born time began.
When I die the universe will end.
And I am dancing too fast to see
I stretch to the end of everything
You cannot see the all of me.

Put your own verse here:
When you were born the universe began.
When you die time will end.
You are dancing too fast for me, too.
You reach beyond the all that is
And I cannot know the all of you.

And you. You put your own verse here.
Yes you. I mean you and you and you.
When you were born, galaxies came to be;
When you die, eternity will end.
And you are dancing so very fast
And you take up all the worlds.
I only know the little bit that flies right past.

And I am all alone in this
I am the only one who exists
For all time, for every space

And you are all alone in this
You are the only one who exists
In all space, for every time

And we are always alone encompassing everything
Always tied with strings, always connected:
I am a pattern made and making
Strings tossed to me, I send strings out
To you, from you, to her, to him, from mom, to dad
To sister, from brother, to aunt, uncle, cousin, lover
From friends, to enemies and their dear ones
And my eternity is unique and dances
And your universe is unique and dances.
Whole galaxies are formed that spin into something,
Whole eons and ages come to be.

This is no place and everywhere
New times are born and die
Here and nowhere eternities create and pass
Where I am is a dance of light
What I am is everywhere

ALICE TEETER

oh oh oh and to be the one who can see it all.

How we connect.

The lightning strikes.

The almost meeting.

The thin line that stretches way across from one to another.

Oh, to see our surprising and beautiful shapes —

To see us all in the fields at play.

Everlasting Chocolate Cake Haiku

Physicists eat cake.
Each takes one half with each bite.
Cake lasts forever.

Ingredients bought by Jim Grimsley and Kathie deNobriga
Cake mixed by Kathie deNobriga and Alice Teeter
Cake baked by Alice Teeter

THE SAVAGE

The savage came in from the woods to sit
in the chairs of big business and learning.
She put on clothes, acquired the habit
of speaking sweetly, softly, and slightly leaning;
She listened with intensity.

She came in from the woods; she had big feet,
her fingernails were cracked, her hands dirty
from digging. Her skin was brown from the heat
of years. She squirmed in her chair, it didn't matter.
She squirmed in her seat, the chair hurt her back,
she smelled like moss roses, she couldn't follow their chatter.

NINE WOMENSONG

Pam, if she lived then,
Pam would be the woman in the woods
and know the secrets;
raising her arms to the moon
with her cats watching.

Caren, if she lived then,
She would ride a horse with wings;
one could catch her with truth,
but never hold her.

Lona, if she lived then,
Lona would make clear water
with leaves from her hands.
One would find her sleeping,
curled in the hollow of a tree.

Mary, if she lived then,
She could become invisible at will
and ride only the wind.
She would never be
in the same place twice.

Carol, if she lived then,
She would sing on clear nights,
and her voice would calm the birds
        before the storm,
and her voice would be the storm.

ALICE TEETER

Deborah, if she lived then,
She would see through walls;
and know the future
    better than the past,
the sun would wait for her to rise.

Lily, if she lived then,
She would be all three:
Child   Maiden   Hag.
From her left hand would come cursing.
with her right she would bless.

Hélène, if she lived then,
She would wander forests
        in bright skirts,
wearing red silk scarves.
They would follow her into a silver sea
        and drown.

Susan, if she lived then,
the air would not move without her.
If She danced in the north,
snow might fall; and in the south,
        warm rain.
Storms would move from the hem of her skirt.

THE 103RD BIRTHDAY OF
EMMA REGINA DeGRAFFENREID SMITH

Great-granddaughter Molly – Annie and Robert's daughter

I was four years old when we came to the Inner Passage.
It's heaven here. I don't remember anything from before.
My favorite things are fishing and blueberry season.
I go alone! Mom says that Granny Em is my first love.
Then Granny Em says "And I'll be your first broken heart."
Hurray, Hurray, Hurray! You're 103 years old today!

Great-grandson Tommy – Annie and Robert's son

Big deal. So she's 103 years old today.
She's just wrinkled and old. It's not like a rite of passage.
When we left Los Angeles it broke my heart.
I'd never even been out of the city before.
I have a girl friend there and we are mad in love.
Plus there's no TV here. I miss baseball season.

Great-grandson Cadmus – Reggie's son

There is no TV here and I miss LA and its one season.
I can't believe Granny Em is 103 years old today.
I thought I would hate it here, but there's things I love.
Last week we saw a bunch of whales out in the Passage!
And I heard there was a tidal wave here once before,
but if we moved back to LA it wouldn't break my heart.

ALICE TEETER

Great-granddaughter Phaedra – Reggie's daughter

If we move back to LA again it won't break my heart.
The absolute worst thing here is the winter season.
I do like this house better than the apartment we were in before.
And it's really nice that we could come over to town today.
Last time we came Tommy ran away, he'd booked his passage.
Oh, I told my Aunt and Granny Em about my new pen-pal love.

Granddaughter Reggie

I told Annie and Granny Em about Lewis, my new love.
I never thought that I'd be willing to risk my heart.
Although these days divorce is like a rite of passage.
I think we'll be married by the end of fishing season.
It would make him happy if we could marry today.
I told him I won't be rushed like I was before.

Grandson-in-law Robert – married to Annie

I told Tommy we are going to do things like before.
You can't go rushing off, leave those you love.
We are going to have a good time here today.
There's a birthday cake with a big blue heart.
Pretty soon we'll start the long winter season
and he'll have to stay. He can't cross the Passage.

Granddaughter Annie

We thought we'd lose Granny Em in the passage over or before.
She is in her winter season, but she has all this love.
It's her strong, strong heart that keeps her with us today.

Great-grandson Pericles Emmanuel – Reggie's son

My dad was my mom's second husband.
He's the one she says is drinking himself to death.
He got mean and violent and we had to get out.
I've talked to him, but I haven't seen him since.
I want to go visit. Mom says "we'll see."
I know if I go back he won't be the same.

Great-grandson Paris – Reggie's son

Nothing on the island ever changes. It's always the same.
I'm glad my mom has found another man to be her husband.
For me there's nowhere to meet people and nothing to see.
I hate it out there and I'm always bored to death.
You'd think we would take the boat over here more since
there's no grocery stores and we're always running out.

Great-granddaughter Ariadne – Reggie's daughter

There's no grocery stores, but I love running out
in the woods for mushrooms. They don't all look the same!
We moved away from LA and it's been great ever since.
I don't miss Creepy Joe – that's what I call mom's last husband.
She says he is trying to drink himself to death.
Whether he does or not we'll have to wait and see.

ALICE TEETER

Great grandson Carleton – Annie and Roberts' son

Whether we can stay here we don't know, we'll have to see.
Mom could lose her job, then we'd have to get out.
I think for Molly to move, it would take death.
It's heaven here for me, too. I'm just the same.
I like the guy that's going to be Reggie's husband.
Maybe he'll come live with us, I mean if and since…

Grandson-in-law-to-be Lewis

I'd be willing to live out there with them, I mean since…
I could probably get to my job from there, we'd have to see.
I'm looking forward to it. I've never been a husband.
I guess if it doesn't work then I'll just get out.
Of course, I mean, she can do the same,
even though we each will promise unto death…

Granddaughter Annie

These kids are going to bug me to death!
I was the one who fought for this job, since
fifty other rangers wanted the same.
For a long time it was wait and see, wait and see,
but then I prevailed and I beat them out!
Got this lighthouse for my kids and husband.

Emma Regina DeGraffenreid Smith

I don't know why I didn't die when I lost my husband.
I almost did. I'm sure I could have pined to death.
Something on the boat ride out here shook me up and out,
got me moving. I haven't stopped since!
There's too much to do and too much to see.
Nothing on the island ever stays the same.

When I lost my husband, I thought it meant death,
but then, we came out here and ever since,
what I look at I see and my days are never the same.

DISMAL FALLS

Past meadows cleared for deer, old apple trees,
sign of homes long gone, down an ancient buffalo trail
turned logging road, funeral path, and then my way;
along the creek, towards Dismal Falls I move.

First, lost on the wrong creek,
then yellow floats up on the sunlight.
Leaves wet beneath my feet,
along the creek signs of fast, high water,
bare rock, twisted trees.
The path along the one cliff narrow;
out through half-bare trees stone rises again
on the far side.

At the foot of the falls, a trickle of water
down one hundred feet. Two kinds of stone on the face.
A pool, and then a run of water beneath the rocks.

Here, the faucet drips from too much cold,
thuds on dirty dishes in the sink.

LUCIFER

I have been Lucifer
beating my wings
on the great gates of Heaven
locked out   abandoned
shut away from love.

I have been the child
who didn't understand
in the man who killed
his lover for leaving
& the woman alone
with the pills in her hand
who banged on the door
wanting love & given cookies
wanting love & fed slaps
wanting love & struck
until striking was all there was

I have been Lucifer
standing with my back to the door
my wings wrapped around me
cast out and uncaring
spitting the vile taste
of Heaven from my mouth.

ALICE TEETER

I have been that murderous thought
that impulse to grab the cat
and throw it in the burning drum...
to secretly smother the child
asleep in the next room...
to strike out with my fists & break
the nose, the cheek, the fingers...

And I have been Lucifer flying over the world
& I have scooped me up like a baby in my arms
& bent my head to listen to me as
I wailed out my sorrow
as I whaled out my anger
as I whispered every thought
every impulse & I have heard me
say it & I will hear me again
& I will say it to you over & over
& I will always make sure
there is someone to hear me knock
who will open the door.

ONE VARIATION ON A THEME

I.

She walked out one night
to take the trash out
and never came back.
Somehow between the door
and the garbage can
she stepped out of line.
She wanders somewhere
with garbage in her hand
exchanging glances with
the trash men
and picking up bottles
no deposit
                no return.

ALICE TEETER

The Woman Who Ate Anger

The woman who ate anger was as big as a house.
She was fat and fatter, dined on anger served up daily
by a husband, children, mother, father,
friend, neighbor, coworker, clerk, self.
She ate it all down.
She grew enormous, moved less and less
until she couldn't fit through the door,
so she lay on her bed,
a pond of flesh flowing over the sides.
The TV cameras filmed her,
the woman who ate anger
weighed a ton.

One day she clenched her jaw against it – ground a "no"
and with her one hand that could still move
pushed away instead of pulled toward.
It wore her out. She slept.

The next day her jaw ground shut,
then opened with a retching sound.
Her arm pushed back harder, both hands clenched,
the bed shook with her effort.
Drenched in sweat, she slept.

She dreamed she unzipped her skin and stepped out.
By the end of the year her legs kicked constantly.
Midway through the next she got up and walked
to the door. They used saws and cut away the frame.
Months later she left the house, and the cameras
filmed her moving with her flesh
hanging like chains from her waist hips ankles and arms.
She walked into the swimming pool and rested,
her fat kept her afloat, high in the water.
All day, every day, she swam back and forth,
soon the distance got shorter.
The TV cameras grew bored and went away.

She swam and started singing.
She sang so loud that the neighbors complained.
She said "Good." "They should complain," and "I don't care."
She swam and sang and the day came
when she left the pool all wrinkled like a prune,
and still singing she danced naked across the lawn.

YOUR MOTHER FROM HER DEATHBED RISES

Your mother from her deathbed rises.
She's happier than you ever remember.
She's going out to meet friends for lunch.
You want to go with her – you've never
seen her like this – all the energy – the joy –
her face alight – you want to be with her.

She tells you that you cannot go with her.
She's excited to see these strangers.
She hasn't seen them for a long time.

She's going alone to meet her friends.
She takes the car even though
she never learned to drive.

AMONG THE BIRDS

Among the birds you wait for
one already sits on your shoulder.
She sings in your ear
sweet songs and terrible:
Enclosing the sound of a high wind,
the sounds you forget,
a child in dusty alleys.
She sings doubt in one ear,
belief in the other.
You always feel her
though sometimes you forget,
when she sings two notes at once,
one from her throat,
one from her belly.
She builds a nest from your hair and roses,
their colors drip down your arm.
When she leaves you
she will scratch you once
and fly away.

ALICE TEETER

Wood Chip Pile

Earthworms congregate,
termites raise young.
It seems a wet ruin
but the center is dry as bone.

MOTH CAUGHT

moth caught
in fine lace curtains
fluttering all day long
then
window open
straight it flies
like knowing
a place to go
yet after a day of living

so many things are changed

33

VIBRATIONS – THE STARS WILL COME DOWN...

For Kathie

SLEEPING GIANT LOVE

My love is a sleeping giant.
You touch her shoulder,
She wakes slowly,
yawns and smiles.

You kiss her cheek.
She lifts her head into the clouds,
Rises humming with you on her arm.

You place your hand on her hips,
her feet move.
She leaps up dancing,
grabs you and spins.

You kiss her lips.
She wakes up roaring,
sweeps you up,
leaps the mountains singing.

Clouds swirl behind her
and collide into thunderstorms.
Trees tiptoe on root tips,
try to regain their balance.
Boulders play leapfrog
in her wake.

ALICE TEETER

FULL MOON WANING

It isn't fair,
dancing with someone else,
wanting you here.

Full moon waning, the night is bright,
the music is moving my feet.
Dancing with someone else,
when it's you I wanted to meet.

You must be true magnetic north.
When you walk in the room my heart,
my heart, like the hands on a compass,
like the hands of a compass, my heart swings.

The sun rises, the moon's still there.
I don't trust it for my guide.
I've been on earth too long,
know so well how east is west
easily lost in a song.

The compass points wherever you are,
my hands move on their own.
The moon is bright, it hides the stars.
I don't trust my eyes, I follow my heart.

The moon rose huge last night,
it filled all the air.
The moon rose so big
and still you weren't there.

Full moon waning, the night is bright,
the music is moving my feet.
Dancing with someone else,
when it's you I wanted to meet.

I think of you, I feel the pull
and my heart, like the hands of a compass,
like the hands on a compass,
my heart swings.

19TH EROTIC BREAKDOWN

You murmur something I cannot quite hear.
Perhaps it is only some innocent question.
The sound of your voice is more than enough.

Inside the car is red felt.
A confusion of smells swarms in the air.
Water beads everywhere.
Your hand is warm on my shoulder.
A brief touch is all.

How far the mind goes on so little.
I do not seem to care.
For a whole day I am lost.
I think of no one else.

Regard Your Heart

Regard your heart. I want it whole,
and I can wait a while.
Regard your heart, you've got mine.
You stole it by your smile.

Calm and lost in a fine-mist feeling,
my head is foggy, barely reeling,
drunk on a light, sweet wine.
I'm floating on the Sargasso Sea
lighting a beacon to guide you to me.

Regard your heart. I want it whole.
I'll take it bit by bit.
Regard your heart, understand,
you took mine with your hands.

Calm, still lost in a slow, slow burning.
My head's on fire, it's turning,
sitting this close to a flame.
I'm rising in a hot air balloon,
I've thrown down a rope to bring you here soon.

Regard your heart. I want it whole.
I can show you how much.
Regard your heart, you've got mine.
You snatched it with your touch.

ALICE TEETER

Calm, but lost in a summer feeling,
my head is clear, but I'm still reeling,
breathing a rare, new air.
High in the clouds when night turns from day,
I'm dropping flares to show you the way.

Regard your heart. I want it whole.
I'll take it bit by bit.
Regard your heart, I've got no choice,
you lifted mine with your voice.

LET US WEAVE

Let us weave our hair together, you and I.
Let us weave a mat to sleep on.
Your hair to pillow our heads,
mine in layers beneath us.

And let us weave a tapestry for walls;
work in feathers floating on water,
shells thick with sand from the beach,
tie in scraps of paper and bits of bright cloth.

Let us braid our hair together, you and I.
Plait one thick rope to climb up with,
a strong cord to swing down.
Twist strings to tie around our fingers.

Let us weave a rug for dancing.
Hoop one for a circle dance,
block one for a square dance,
one in a zig-zag
and one for a promenade.

Let us weave our hair together, you and I.
Let us weave a mat to sleep on.
Your hair to pillow our heads,
mine in layers around us.

ALICE TEETER

MY LITTLE OYSTER

Oh my little oyster,
When I think about you,
My mouth starts to water,
My mouth feels the dew.

Oh my little oyster,
When I think about your pearl,
My fingers get greedy,
My toes start to curl.

Oh my little oyster,
When I remember your charms,
I leap to my feet
(It causes great alarm).

Oh little oyster,
When we swim in the sea,
Do you like the salty water
Half as much as me?

OH YES

I could feel cheated
     oh yes
I could feel unwanted
          unneeded
     oh yes
I could feel left
        bereft
I could feel mad
      very sad
    yes
and missing you
after what may as well be years
and what I learned from you
I cannot use with you
who I learned it for
    yes
I knew how much I had
    yes
and how fast it would go
    yes
    oh yes
I could go on
singing the loved and lost songs
I loved

oh yes
but it didn't work out right
yes, yes, yes
not quite right
ooh all those funky blues songs
those radio pop songs
oh we lost everything – turned ourselves
inside out
left everything behind
like people leave a haunted house
food on the table and toys scattered
in the yard

MIDNIGHT – AFTER THE BALL (1994)

After they danced
the bold and daring prince
turned into a shy and timid frog
declared love and sat.

After they kissed
the brave and beautiful princess
turned into a tiny bird
sang nervously and fled.

ALICE TEETER

November

I am thinking about joining the stones.
I am thinking of laying my head in Her lap.
The birds fly over, they fly over so high
and I have known concrete so long
that wooden steps are nice,
covered in grass and cracked rusty nails.

I had a reason last night, not desperation;
a reason, not desolate, not lacking.
I can't remember today, but the feeling's still here.
A hill with stones and a cradle; on top of a wall
keeping back the ocean,
looking at crabs and broken bleached shells.

Sonnet II

I was out walking and the stars
were so numerous and bright
that I could have grabbed one
and not diminished the light.
And the wind was so sharp and fresh
that I shook to feel
the air slide into my lungs
to there refresh and heal,
but I shook not only from the wind
it was seeing you again that made
me feel the emptiness of time
and how much memories can fade.
     I am so full of emptiness
     that I can drink no more.

ALICE TEETER

DUST

There is a mouthful of dust in my smile.
I would dance until I drop,
tear out my heart
that you are not dazzled,
that you are not amazed
not moved when it is you I see.

You are the stone I carry in my mouth.
I speak clearly and polish the words.
I forget and you remind me.
I move and walk in other rooms,
my heart whole and wholly mine;
then I see you in the kitchen
sitting in the afternoon sun.
Your hands rest on the table.

You are the eyelash in my vision.
I sit on the porch in the evening
laying out my motives before me,
a deck of cards, the tarot of my desire.
Your back is to me.
Are we looking at the same wisp
of dandelion spreading out in the breeze?
or is it my eyes only
that take in that scene?

Yes, you are the mouthful of dust
that is in my smile.
I smile just the same.

18TH CENTURY SPANISH LOVE POEM

When we met again in the marketplace
after all those years, I saw that the angels
still danced in a line between us.

While we stood before one another the sun emerged
even though the rain did not cease and
all the drops turned to gems and fire
that fell around us as we spoke.

My friends knew who you were immediately.
They laughed at me the rest of the day
because whatever they said to me
I answered with your name.

All that day and the next I sang
and my feet danced wherever I went.
I could not hush my heart nor still my soul.
That night I found myself beneath your open window.
I called your name and you appeared.

Your refusal to walk with me
in the cool of that evening through the arbor,
your declaration that you still forsake love,
even your closing the window and withdrawing,
none of that has quieted my ardor.

Love has not forsaken you.
It lives in my heart and sings your name,
and the angels still dance.

SACRED HEART

Look. One would think it frozen,
this expanse of white emptiness, iced-over and cold.
Do not try to walk here.

If you step out onto it you will find that it is white hot.

In cracks through the crust you can smell the black syrup
filled with rotting parts of animals: birds' wings, shrunken,
clung to by bits of feathers; bones of a dog,
muscle still strung here and there along its length;
intestines rolling with the boil.

A few places, very few & far between, contain a glimpse,
a place where you may lift back the dried-out crust
and view the pure, pink-red core beneath.

But, indeed, sometimes it is cold
and a voice will wail from across the field.
It sounds like a cry for the dead.

PAGODA HEART

I want my heart to be swept clean
like an oriental temple.
Polished wood floors, rice paper walls
translucent with light and air.
A view of the rock garden
shimmering in the afternoon sun.
The only sound a distant gong
or wind through bamboo.

What I have is a heart cluttered with debris.
Last week's lasagna left out on the counter.
All the dishes piled in the sink.
Dirty and clean clothes clumped together.
Papers, magazines, apple cores ink stained;
fruit flies hover over the desk.

I want a heart swept clean
new and open with air and light.

I'd take a heart with one room like a pagoda
The rest of the house a chaos of creativity.

ALICE TEETER

INVITATION...

we could call ourselves creators of another universe
spinning worlds that dance out complex patterns
enlarging the galaxy to fit into our hands

we could say we are present in the present
we could say that being present
in the present is a present

we could say it is a gift

it could be a research project, a collaborative study
recording the effects of time and distance
on gravity and light, an ongoing data stream

we could say we have gone fishing
we could call it participating
in a catch and release program

we could be the fish we catch, the fish that get away

we could call it a Tahitian vacation
a Roman holiday
a Grand Tour of Europe

we could say we are skimming stones
we could say we are skipping large flat stones
over the glassy surface of a lake

we could say we are stones skipping

ALICE TEETER

SAY YES

Say Yes
Step off into this unknown
Into this marvelous and terrible Yes

Yes to unknowing, Yes
Fling your arms wide to Yes

Be light and say Yes
Say Yes softly in a whisper

Float on Yes
Carry Yes like a feather you find floating
That the wind will take away
Blow Yes like a dandelion seed
Scatter it to the winds

And me   I say Yes waiting for your Yes
Leaning in and watching for it floating down
A maple seed on the breeze spiraling
Wisps of white floating across my field of vision
My ears are listening for that whisper

You are standing on the sweet spot of the stage
Your voice will carry for eons and leagues
In your softest song say Yes to me
I hear you from this thousand miles away

HEART STRING THEORY

What is this place in my heart
that vibrates to the sound of your voice?
Was it always there, a long cord embedded
in the wall of the chamber waiting to pull free,
set to moving, glistening red and thrumming?
Or did it form out of thin air? Your voice spoke,
the vibration turned to this gut-wound string
and spanned this space now open and singing.

When a heart wakes up – when the ice has broken –
    when the fire is flowing –
What is it that sounds – what is it that pulls – that vibrates?
What is this place in my heart that sounds to the ring of your voice?

ALICE TEETER

MYSTERY V.8

we are a mystery
flaming questions
burning in the dark

atom A atom C once touched
now a thousand light years apart
one changes shape
the other changes too
in the same instant
both are transformed

Even now I carry you and toss you up in the air
you are a laughing woman   I catch you lightly as a breath
I float a foot off the ground   slowly revolve
up and down   head over heels until it is you
who has me in her arms and I am a laughing woman too

the hologram of
two red rose vines
intertwined
cut in half
is still two red rose vines
intertwined
doubled

no matter how many times
a knife or scissors or teeth
rips it in two
each piece is the whole
down too small to see

why did we?
how will we?
what now?

viewed from a distance
from this angle I look like me
I see myself straight on
viewed from there
from that vantage you look like you
I see you from the back
I notice that when I turn
you turn at the same time
when I raise my arm hello
your arm raises in greeting
to someone in front of you
who I cannot see from here
I wave at myself
hello
you wave ahead of you
hello

61

here is still the smile I love
the fingers   that little one
the hands   the stronger arms
the breath   the body   the spirit

who are we?
how is it that we?
what does it mean?

the feel of the earth
beneath my back
the blue sky overhead
you on my left
the world moving

we are a mystery
a flaming question
burning in the dark

I leave the questions burning
flaming in the dark sky
and in the daylight visible
just there suspended in air

sometimes that is enough
sometimes that is not enough
sometimes the only thing I know to do

SUMMER OF LOVE SERIES

1

THE RED IN THAT TREE
BY THE RED IN THAT TREE

The body does not know the difference
between awake and sleeping.

In this world we are sailing in a small boat on a wide bay
to the house we have rented for the summer
on the end of the spit that swings way out
away from the mainland. It takes us all day.
This is the only means we have of getting there –
this journey that began on the breath of the morning.
It is not that far, and we are inept sailors
even with our sturdy brown legs and strong arms
holding rudder and boom steady as we go.
Just in case, we have stowed a pair of oars.

On this day, the sky is blue with white clouds,
the air breezy and cool but warmed by the sun.
We start out singing, in silence to ourselves,
then one of us – yes, it is you – sings aloud,
and we both join in louder and louder until
we sing, then laugh, the sound booming across the water
above the air. Midway across, the gentle wind gives out.
The land has paused before the afternoon's inhale
and we sit quiet and eat our dark brown bread,
our bright yellow cheese and violet grapes.

ALICE TEETER

Drowsing, we sit at either end, our bare feet touching
around the mast, the anchor out to keep from drifting.
The gulls that came to have lunch with us have flown.
The water is glassy calm, the air hot and bright,
the white clouds are building high above us.
Once in a while I point out some shape forming
and you sometimes agree and sometimes you say no
It looks more like the face of someone you know.
Not an elephant at all, but a dear face in the sky.
In the silence we suddenly realize how late it is
How late we are and how much further we have to go.

Because there is no breeze to send us on our way
Because we do not know when the wind will rise again
Because it seems suddenly so late and so far
We fold up the sail and put out the oars
You on the left and me on the right
And it takes a while for us to figure it out
At first we go in circles or veer wildly off course
But after a bit we are heading the right way
And the oars make swirls in the water
We are heading right into the sun as it sinks lower and lower.

We are singing again, you and I
Only this time it is work songs we know
We take turns leading the other
To keep our pace up and to keep time
At first we make up words to fit our work
"I've been rowing in a sailboat

all the live long day" and
"John Henry was a sailboat rowing man…"
but after a while we are handsore and tired
and all we can do is keep rowing
and the songs trail off into the wake of the boat
and we row in silence as the sun sets.

In the golden light of dusk we arrive
Sliding up to the stone landing
Oars benched, I grab the belay pin
And hold on, threading the rope through
Praying I am using the right knot
To keep the boat secure
I hold on to the railing as you step out
Bare feet on the wet stones of the pier
I hand you your small suitcase
The black one with the rope handle,
then my brown bag with a worn leather grip
Then the knapsacks with our supper
You lean down and hold the boat
As I climb out to stand beside you.

There is a stone bench set back a little ways.
We make for that, wobbly on our feet,
unused to the feel of such a solid floor.
We watch the sun go down, feel the inhale
of the land moving across our faces.
Before the last little bit of light is gone,

ALICE TEETER

we rise, grab our bags and trudge
on shaky legs up the stone stairs
to the unlit house with bougainvilleas
glowing in the dark by the door.

2

THAT WHITE CLOUD IN THE SKY
BY THAT WHITE CLOUD IN THE SKY

between walking in the mind
or walking a sandy road.

We bandage our hands by lantern light,
our simple supper, outside toilet and wash,
When we fall into bed together, we sink,
the ropes underneath the mattress give way
and we are too tired and sore to care as the night air
begins to move over us through the room.
We shiver all night and cling to one another,
Sharing the one pillow, listening to the sea, the wind,
my breath in your ear, your arm falls asleep holding me
in the strangest house either of us has ever seen.

The sun rises straight through the window,
warms your back and we turn to face the light,
watch as the light plays on the water
and lights up the room around us, the rough wooden furniture,
the hooks hammered into the stone walls,
shutters we did not see the night before,
a painting of flowers hangs over the window,
a high shelf with blankets and a second pillow,
and I notice right before you say the same thing,
that the walls are carved from living rock.

69   ALICE TEETER

This is a house full of doorways and windows,
open to the east and west and south, solid to the north,
a house carved from a boulder on the end of the spit,
covered in bougainvilleas and swept clean by the sea and air.
We rise with difficulty, our blistered hands and tender arms
Little match for the sagging ropes. You say you'd never felt so sore.
I use my legs and feet to propel you up and out of bed
We laugh then, because there is no one to push me
and laughing is the only thing we know to do
as you pull me up and we begin our first day.

You find the fresh eggs and yogurt on the kitchen window
Placed there before dawn, the eggs still warm, and a loaf of bread
This is our breakfast then, we sit wrapped in blankets on the terrace
The wide ocean to our right, the mainland far to our left
The sea gulls float up in the sky, and cry in the breeze
The day is clear and sunny and blue and we are barefoot
bare-legged and young. You grab a fishing pole off the wall
I grab a basket down. You head west. I head east
We wave to one another across the widening spit as we both
Thread rocks north toward fish and market on this morning.

I look at the mountains ahead of me in the distance
The ones that isolate this narrow spit of land
They rise jagged and white capped up into the clouds
And I wonder who lives up there and what they do each day.
You look into the water by your side or ahead
And I see you spot other fisherfolk at play in the surf
You call over to me about how barren the ocean floor seems
Compared to where you grew up and fished before.
I am making lunch when you come home, you
Swing a line of fish that you use to slap my thigh.

This afternoon we tighten the ropes on the bed
And bounce up and down on the mattress
Napping and tickling and loving as the ropes
Slowly settle back to their former slackness
And our arms work out their soreness
Our hands forget to feel blistered
Until we sleep sticky in the afternoon heat
Silent in our own dreams as the afternoon pauses
I dream about sailing with the wind blowing my hair
You dream about the city and working at your desk.

ALICE TEETER

Then you go off to explore the foothills
At the base of the mountains beyond the little town.
I sit in a chair on the terrace and write letters.
You find a butterfly bush so big and covered
With butterflies that you know it must be god.
You pick up three smooth stones from the stream
And carry them home in your pocket to me
You come around the corner of the house
I tell you to look, look up at the sky
Angels are carding the clouds getting ready to weave.

3

THE STARS IN THE SKY
BY THE STARS IN THE SKY

Between dreaming of flying and flying

I grow restless first, and pace the terrace and house
I feel confined, bored, jumpy and mean.
You are happy still fishing in the morning,
loving in the afternoon, exploring the town
which has suddenly grown too small for me.
This narrow spit of land feels too closed in.
I keep looking at the mountains to expand.
Finally you take pity on me and tell me
we should hike up to the inn you'd heard about,
the one way up in the mountains, two days away.

I bless your generous heart and willing legs,
so ready to be off that I run around the house,
packing our meager belongings, ready to go
before you are barely finished speaking.
You take it in good stride and we are off
and the day is beautiful again, the sky wide.
It isn't until we leave the village behind
and are in the rolling hills that I think
about sleeping outside one night unsheltered
and wonder what beasts might find us as we rest.

ALICE TEETER

I stop, trembling in the narrow track,
afraid to go on, unwilling to go back and you,
you laugh at me, you laugh at me,
and say there haven't been wolves, or bears, seen
on the spit or in these mountains for a century,
which makes my heart light and heavy at once
and I walk on angry at you for laughing,
lighthearted to feel safe on the trek,
heavy at heart for the desolation of the wild,
looking forward to a night in the open air.

We walk until dusk and my anger melts.
My sadness fades into the sunset and the feathers
in my heart sink slowly, weighed by the dew.
We sit and eat some bread, plums and yellow cheese,
on a flat rock in the middle of the creek,
and watch the sun sink behind the hills.

You find a spot on the other side of the creek,
flat and open, luxurious with long grass.
You unroll the blanket and we sink down,
me commenting it is softer than our other bed.

When I lie back and put my arms out for you
I look up and suddenly shout, I stare at the stars
spread out like storm clouds across the sky.
You are alarmed and ask what is wrong.

All I can do is point up at the heavens.
You say it is the Milky Way that you've seen often
growing up in the country and while you were in France.
I am speechless and so sad for my childhood
of too much light and thinking about my nieces
and nephews growing up now without a chance to see.

I cannot sleep. I keep disturbing yours,
looking around the bowl of the sky, at every star,
looking for Orion, the Bear, I ask you
if that's the North Star, and what is that one over there.
I hold up my arm to try and see which way the stars
are turning and watch as the night deepens.
More and more stars appear until my eyes
are glittery and I can't tell if they are open or closed
or whether I am awake or dreaming in your arms.

ALICE TEETER

4

THE BLUE IN THE SKY
BY THE BLUE IN THE SKY

Awake or asleep the dream is real
The stars shine on in the blue

As the sun is coming up, I fall asleep.
You sleep on, too, and the air grows warm
around us and the tall grass slides over us,
leans over and tickles our noses and we stir,
drowsy as the light comes in red through our eyelids.
Small bugs begin searching the hair on our arms.
One particular slender stalk of grass
is finally too insistent for you and you
brush it aside with exasperation and rise.

It takes your tongue in my ear to wake me.
I push myself out of the blanket of grass
stagger to the creek and wash my face,
the icy water serving as coffee and bath
to clear the fog of stars from my head.
You are stretching, standing on the flat rock,
holding up your arms to the rising sun.
All I can see is your shadow
inside a halo of yellow light.

How slyly you pull from your bag
a bar of chocolate and you do your best
to pretend that you are hiding it from me,
and I do my best to pretend that I've caught you out.
We wrestle for the chocolate as if our lives
depend on it, you being just enough taller
to keep it out of reach over your head –
just enough stronger that I can't get to it
until I take you down, folding your legs with mine.

My revenge is to turn you into chocolate,
I smear your neck, your belly, your thighs
with the sticky, melting bar and lick it off
competing with the ants to see who gets the most.
My greedy mouth wins the field and then you sleep.
I have my eyes closed in the noonday sun listening
to the birds singing overhead and the bees
in the clover nearby – so busy, so busy.
I wonder at how hard it is to remember the stars.

I use a cupful of cold water from the stream
to wake and wash you, the waking works
much better than the washing and you're up.
I do not want to go, but it won't do to stay
so we are off, walking uphill now, up and up,
for the rest of the day. I admire your brown legs
ahead of me on the slope and when we pause
to rest, I notice the ever widening vista,
the spit opening out behind us and the sea.

ALICE TEETER

You talk about dancing, about the rhythm, the beat
You talk about the Sufi's dancing and ballet.
You talk about the beauty of movement and
You move your arms and skip lightly
To show me what you mean and I understand
Only a glimmer of what you say but your movements
go through me like a drumbeat or the low note
Of a big horn blowing out across the air
And I think that you are dance itself.

Late in the afternoon we walk down
Into a valley and then begin to climb again
I ask you how much farther.
You say you thought it was this peak
The one we are climbing and we stop,
Eat the last of our bread and watch
As the sun turns the sky red on the horizon
And the blue deepens above us.
It is the bluest blue we've ever seen.

5

A BOWL OF CLOUDS
BY A BOWL OF CLOUDS

The body cannot tell apart
What is imagined and what is real

We reach the peak at dusk. You would have
Walked right by in the dark, but I stop
To shake a rock from my shoe and notice
Stepping stone shapes covered with fine dust.
They lead to a building closed and shuttered.
We knock and when no one answers
We walk in calling out louder and louder
No one answers or appears and fine dust
Swirls in our flashlight beams as we rummage.

We choose a room on the end and open the shutters
The back door leads to a long porch and we sit out there
I wonder why no one is here and you are silent.
We look out across the dark valley that falls away
below the porch and see the stars coming out
as deep night falls. We sweep out the room in the dark
And shake the blankets and pillows out over the rail.
The dust is so deep we move slowly to keep it still
You are bewildered. I am hungry. The night seems very long.

ALICE TEETER

An hour before dawn I give up sleeping and go out
onto the porch and stretch, doing my best to still my mind
and my empty belly in the quiet darkness.
You rise with the sun and join me, stretching
like you do for dance, using the rail as a bar,
Your bare feet catch the first light as it
spreads in front of us over the valley.
As you move I look down into the bowl,
It is full of gray and white clouds swirling.

We stand silently, arms wrapped around one another.
Watching the patterns in the valley as the clouds
dance together and roll smoothing out the curls.
A cool breeze comes up and your hair
Blows into my face and I feel perfumed and adorned
By the wisps as they tickle and lightly touch
And I know the moment is passing at the same time
All of me wants it to last forever and I know
You feel the same. We want the same moment.

When it is light enough we open all the windows
And search the place. We find olives and bread
Tucked away tightly in ceramic jars.
We refill our canteens from the pump
By the front door. I am for staying another night.
You are for leaving right away and we fight
The first fight of the summer and it is hard
Hard because the bitter words are not about that day
They are about the days soon to come when we will part.

What ends our argument is a shock
The ground shakes and we step into the road
I am sure it is lasting forever, you time it from the first jolt
To the last shudder and say "5 seconds"
I have no way to argue and no passion for it
We carefully make our way around the hostel
Look for signs of weakness and cracks
I go in and get our things
You are the one who packs our food and water.

We stand a last time on the porch looking out across the valley
The breeze shifts and blows the clouds away
And we understand why there is no one here
As we look down into a crater venting steam.
I know your argument should win the day
We leave without a word to one another
Heartsick and footsore as we trudge
Down the road, back the way we came
Where everything now has changed.

ALICE TEETER

6

A REFLECTION OF LIGHT
BY THE REFLECTION OF LIGHT

What never happened and
What is true.

The summer ends early, our time cut short.
We flee the spit of land, mustered out by troops
in front of a lava flow – a rain of hot ash
that comes pouring down. The narrow strip of land
destroyed by what had made it – our summer home
pushed into the sea, the village covered over.
Even the little boat we'd sailed out in is gone,
burned into the water by the rain of fire,
the red flowers by the door turned to cinder.

We are long gone by then. We leave with all the others
holding hands on the ship that takes us away.
Several times you hold my hand up to your face.
More than once I kiss your little finger,
as we sit rocking in the galley where they stow us.
We are lucky, we have our knapsacks and our lives.
We've left nothing behind there except for the book
that fell out of my bag unnoticed on the way down
Or maybe in the last dash out of the house of living rock.

We make our way back to the city you live in.
The one I can't live in and can't bear to leave.
We take the night train across those miles
The last lightness of summer already turning to metal
Silent together, taking turns sleeping across the seat
Your lap pillows my head, then mine yours.
We smell smoke all the way there
And see fire every time we close our eyes.
Crossing the mountains we are both wide awake.

That last night I spend with you there is no sleep,
We are in your bed beneath those factory windows
the city sky dark and all the lights in your one room ablaze
reflecting off the ceiling-high panes, one panel open
to let in the autumn air and noise from the street.
You grab my left knee and say it is yours

I agree that it is. I tell you that
your little finger on your right hand and your beautiful
feet are mine. You call me greedy and say they are.

All night we hold each other in the misery of parting.
We have stopped our fight, the energy tapped out
By the distances too great and the directions
too opposite to go on the same way together.

ALICE TEETER

You hold yourself above me
The light moves down your body as you rise
Suspended, looking at me looking at you
and I try so hard to inhale every molecule,
taste every atom and and hope to keep them in my memory.

The only aroma of you is you. The only sight of your eyes
Is the sight of your eyes. The only sound of your voice
is your voice. The only feel of your skin is the feel of your skin.
The only curve of your neck is the curve of your neck.
The only shape of your head beneath my hands is
The shape of your head beneath my hands, your hair
Falling forward over your face, red gold and dark.
You are not here now and I am not there now.
There is no trace of you here.

I reach up and turn off the light over the bed
Just as the sun first peeks down the street.
I sit up, you curl around me and I reach back
To run my hand along your spine down your legs
We are both trembling as we rise, silently,
You make coffee I can't drink and hand me
A piece of toast I can't eat and it is time
I kiss you and hug you and kiss you
And go out the door like I'd never been there.

At the end of the street I look back at your window
I wait until I see you move forward. I can barely
see you – a dim shape behind the darkened glass.
We look at one another across the air.
Your raised hand presses the windowpane.
I raise my hand and wave just as the sun
comes full around the corner and you are gone
in a reflection of light.
I turn the corner and disappear.

It has only been a little time, it has been forever
since we parted – days, months, years, always.
Every now and then I hear your voice
across the miles of phone lines and the joy is the same,
the grace, the gladness in my heart to hear you speak
and to talk to you and the price I pay is the same each time
the sorrow afterwards. That once your voice fades
you are gone again and I am not with you
and I am blinded anew by that brilliant reflection of light.

ALICE TEETER

Atomic Lineage

Maybe a billion of your atoms recognize
a billion atoms in the one you love and know
that once you two were one thing before decay
and dispersal swept you across the universe.

Maybe you were the sweeper on the steps
that led up to the Acropolis when it was new,
or a straw in the broom that pushed dirt around the yard
in a village by the Nile, or one mote in the dust stirred up
that one particular afternoon by a thunderstorm
as it swept across the Great Plains.

You could have been the meteorite that flared in the sky
twenty thousand years ago – burning down to nothing –
becoming atoms flying – becoming air and water –
becoming nitrogen and helium – becoming new –
dispersing across the face of the earth.

Maybe our atoms know each other
wanting to be that one remembered thing
finding that the only dance now is gravity
and light always an infinite space apart.

CELL PHONE CALLING

your cell phone left a message on my cell phone
last week
perhaps it was only a last desperate attempt
to connect
as you deleted my name and number
from your list

it was the sound of a modem attempting
to log on
or of a fax machine as it tries to find
a signal
there were no words – only static, swirls
and beeps

maybe my cell phone sent a reply back
some sounds
saying I miss you
in the electric buzz along the wire
I miss you and the words that once flew
connecting us

ALICE TEETER

THE PARTY

It rains in her kitchen – it's open to the sky – a screen for a ceiling.
Even though you've been feuding ever since they moved in
they are generous neighbors, they invite you to their party
you are mostly strangers, this woman and her children.

She walks in and sees you in the middle of her kitchen laughing
your bare feet her red tile floor,
raindrops pouring down across everything.
She moves to you. You kiss her twice on the mouth.
You are hers forever.

She sweeps you up into her arms –
you realize how tall she is, how strong –
she carries you up near the lights, back to the party.

WHEN IT HAPPENS TO YOU…

When it happens to you the stars will come down
flood down through the top of your head –
their light will fill you up completely.

You will walk vibrating through the dark
    of a soft summer night
in and out of shadows – past tents strung with lights –
men and women laughing and singing.

You will pass a few people in the dark.
You love them instantly and completely –
star's light shining on them all.

You will lie wide awake all night
that tremor running through you –
while the air moves from the open window across you.

At dawn you will rise up refreshed and go walking.
You will finally know what it is –
you will finally be ready.

ALICE TEETER

Acknowledgments

Some of the poems in *When it happens to you . . .* have been published previously. "Dream 1: My mother writes poetry," "The Woman Who Ate Anger," "One Variation on a Theme," "10 year old dancing," "Poem for Ellen," "She had a beige childhood," "The Savage," "Nine Womensong," "Dismal Falls," "Sleeping Giant Love," "18th Century Spanish Love Poem," "Say Yes," "Sacred Heart," "Pagoda Heart," "Heart String Theory," "Everlasting Chocolate Cake Haiku," and "String Theory" appeared in *String Theory,* winner of the Georgia Poetry Society's Charles B. Dickson Memorial Chapbook competition for 2008, published by the Georgia Poetry Society, copyright © 2008 by Alice Teeter. Thanks to the family of Charles B. Dickson and to the Georgia Poetry Society for publishing this book.

"The 103rd birthday of Emma Regina DeGraffenreid Smith" was published in the Winter 2009 issue of *Per Contra, The International Journal of the Arts, Literature and Ideas* **www.percontra.net**. Thanks to Per Contra and Miriam N. Kotzin for publishing this poem.

"She had a beige childhood," "One Variation on a Theme," "moth caught," "oh yes," and "She walked through the door" also appeared in *20 CLASS A,* published by friends of the author in 1975, copyright © 1975 by Alice Teeter. Grateful thanks to my friends.

Thanks to my early teachers: Phyllis Gilbert, Blair Ray, the poet Peter Meinke and to the VWA and the Webster's writing group.

Many thanks to poet Lewis Turco for writing *The Book of Forms: A Handbook of Poetics,* also known as "The Poet's Bible."

ALICE TEETER was born in Winter Haven, Florida and grew up writing poetry. She is currently collaborating with performance artist Priscilla Smith on a community-based project that explores the intersections between science and art. She co-leads 'Improvoetry' workshops with producer/director/performer/creativity coach Lesly Fredman, using improvisation techniques as poetic inspiration and poetry as a springboard for further improvisation. Alice is a member of Alternate ROOTS, a service organization for artists doing community-based work in the Southeast. She is also a member of the Artist Conference Network, a national coaching community for people doing creative work. She works as a graphic production artist for a marketing services company and lives in Pine Lake, Georgia with her partner Kathie deNobriga.

Printed in the United States
214513BV00001B/6/P

9 781932 842357